Password Book

Belongs to: _____

Name:_____

User:_____

Password:_____

Email:_____

Name:_____

User:_____

Password:_____

Email:_____

Name:_____

User:_____

Password:_____

Email:_____

Name:_____

User:_____

Password:_____

Email:_____

Name:_____

User:_____

Password:_____

Email:_____

Name:_____

User:_____

Password:_____

Email:_____

Name:_____

User:_____

Password:_____

Email:_____

Name:_____

User:_____

Password:_____

Email:_____

Name:_____

User:_____

Password:_____

Email:_____

Name:_____

User:_____

Password:_____

Email:_____

Name:_____

User:_____

Password:_____

Email:_____

Name:_____

User:_____

Password:_____

Email:_____

Name:_____

User:_____

Password:_____

Email:_____

Name:_____

User:_____

Password:_____

Email:_____

Name:_____

User:_____

Password:_____

Email:_____

Name:_____

User:_____

Password:_____

Email:_____

Name:_____

User:_____

Password:_____

Email:_____

Name:_____

User:_____

Password:_____

Email:_____

Name:_____

User:_____

Password:_____

Email:_____

Name:_____

User:_____

Password:_____

Email:_____

Name:_____

User:_____

Password:_____

Email:_____

Name:_____

User:_____

Password:_____

Email:_____

Name:_____

User:_____

Password:_____

Email:_____

Name:_____

User:_____

Password:_____

Email:_____

Name:_____

User:_____

Password:_____

Email:_____

Name:_____

User:_____

Password:_____

Email:_____

Name:_____

User:_____

Password:_____

Email:_____

Name:_____

User:_____

Password:_____

Email:_____

Name:_____

User:_____

Password:_____

Email:_____

Name:_____

User:_____

Password:_____

Email:_____

Name:_____

User:_____

Password:_____

Email:_____

Name:_____

User:_____

Password:_____

Email:_____

Name:_____

User:_____

Password:_____

Email:_____

Name:_____

User:_____

Password:_____

Email:_____

Name:_____

User:_____

Password:_____

Email:_____

Name:_____

User:_____

Password:_____

Email:_____

Name:_____

User:_____

Password:_____

Email:_____

Name:_____

User:_____

Password:_____

Email:_____

Name:_____

User:_____

Password:_____

Email:_____

Name:_____

User:_____

Password:_____

Email:_____

Name:_____

User:_____

Password:_____

Email:_____

Name:_____

User:_____

Password:_____

Email:_____

Name:_____

User:_____

Password:_____

Email:_____

Name:_____

User:_____

Password:_____

Email:_____

Name:_____

User:_____

Password:_____

Email:_____

Name:_____

User:_____

Password:_____

Email:_____

Name:_____

User:_____

Password:_____

Email:_____

Name:_____

User:_____

Password:_____

Email:_____

Name:_____

User:_____

Password:_____

Email:_____

Name:_____

User:_____

Password:_____

Email:_____

Name:_____

User:_____

Password:_____

Email:_____

Name:_____

User:_____

Password:_____

Email:_____

Name:_____

User:_____

Password:_____

Email:_____

Name:_____

User:_____

Password:_____

Email:_____

Name:_____

User:_____

Password:_____

Email:_____

Name:_____

User:_____

Password:_____

Email:_____

Name:_____

User:_____

Password:_____

Email:_____

Name:_____

User:_____

Password:_____

Email:_____

Name:_____

User:_____

Password:_____

Email:_____

Name:_____

User:_____

Password:_____

Email:_____

Name:_____

User:_____

Password:_____

Email:_____

Name:_____

User:_____

Password:_____

Email:_____

Name:_____

User:_____

Password:_____

Email:_____

Name:_____

User:_____

Password:_____

Email:_____

Name:_____

User:_____

Password:_____

Email:_____

Name:_____

User:_____

Password:_____

Email:_____

Name:_____

User:_____

Password:_____

Email:_____

Name:_____

User:_____

Password:_____

Email:_____

Name:_____

User:_____

Password:_____

Email:_____

Name:_____

User:_____

Password:_____

Email:_____

Name:_____

User:_____

Password:_____

Email:_____

Name:_____

User:_____

Password:_____

Email:_____

Name:_____

User:_____

Password:_____

Email:_____

Name:_____

User:_____

Password:_____

Email:_____

Name:_____

User:_____

Password:_____

Email:_____

Name:_____

User:_____

Password:_____

Email:_____

Name:_____

User:_____

Password:_____

Email:_____

Name:_____

User:_____

Password:_____

Email:_____

Name:_____

User:_____

Password:_____

Email:_____

Name:_____

User:_____

Password:_____

Email:_____

Name:_____

User:_____

Password:_____

Email:_____

Name:_____

User:_____

Password:_____

Email:_____

Name:_____

User:_____

Password:_____

Email:_____

Name:_____

User:_____

Password:_____

Email:_____

Name:_____

User:_____

Password:_____

Email:_____

Name:_____

User:_____

Password:_____

Email:_____

Name:_____

User:_____

Password:_____

Email:_____

Name:_____

User:_____

Password:_____

Email:_____

Name:_____

User:_____

Password:_____

Email:_____

Name:_____

User:_____

Password:_____

Email:_____

Name:_____

User:_____

Password:_____

Email:_____

Name:_____

User:_____

Password:_____

Email:_____

Name:_____

User:_____

Password:_____

Email:_____

Name:_____

User:_____

Password:_____

Email:_____

Name:_____

User:_____

Password:_____

Email:_____

Name:_____

User:_____

Password:_____

Email:_____

Name:_____

User:_____

Password:_____

Email:_____

Name:_____

User:_____

Password:_____

Email:_____

Name:_____

User:_____

Password:_____

Email:_____

Name:_____

User:_____

Password:_____

Email:_____

Name:_____

User:_____

Password:_____

Email:_____

Name:_____

User:_____

Password:_____

Email:_____

Name:_____

User:_____

Password:_____

Email:_____

Name:_____

User:_____

Password:_____

Email:_____

Name:_____

User:_____

Password:_____

Email:_____

Name:_____

User:_____

Password:_____

Email:_____

Name:_____

User:_____

Password:_____

Email:_____

Name:_____

User:_____

Password:_____

Email:_____

Name:_____

User:_____

Password:_____

Email:_____

Name:_____

User:_____

Password:_____

Email:_____

Name:_____

User:_____

Password:_____

Email:_____

Name:_____

User:_____

Password:_____

Email:_____

Name:_____

User:_____

Password:_____

Email:_____

Name:_____

User:_____

Password:_____

Email:_____

Name:_____

User:_____

Password:_____

Email:_____

Name:_____

User:_____

Password:_____

Email:_____

Name:_____

User:_____

Password:_____

Email:_____

Name:_____

User:_____

Password:_____

Email:_____

Name:_____

User:_____

Password:_____

Email:_____

Name:_____

User:_____

Password:_____

Email:_____

Name:_____

User:_____

Password:_____

Email:_____

Name:_____

User:_____

Password:_____

Email:_____

Name:_____

User:_____

Password:_____

Email:_____

Name:_____

User:_____

Password:_____

Email:_____

Name:_____

User:_____

Password:_____

Email:_____

Name:_____

User:_____

Password:_____

Email:_____

Name:_____

User:_____

Password:_____

Email:_____

Name:_____

User:_____

Password:_____

Email:_____

Name:_____

User:_____

Password:_____

Email:_____

Name:_____

User:_____

Password:_____

Email:_____

Name:_____

User:_____

Password:_____

Email:_____

Name:_____

User:_____

Password:_____

Email:_____

Name:_____

User:_____

Password:_____

Email:_____

Name:_____

User:_____

Password:_____

Email:_____

Name:_____

User:_____

Password:_____

Email:_____

Name:_____

User:_____

Password:_____

Email:_____

Name:_____

User:_____

Password:_____

Email:_____

Name:_____

User:_____

Password:_____

Email:_____

Name:_____

User:_____

Password:_____

Email:_____

Name:_____

User:_____

Password:_____

Email:_____

Name:_____

User:_____

Password:_____

Email:_____

Name:_____

User:_____

Password:_____

Email:_____

Name:_____

User:_____

Password:_____

Email:_____

Name:_____

User:_____

Password:_____

Email:_____

Name:_____

User:_____

Password:_____

Email:_____

Name:_____

User:_____

Password:_____

Email:_____

Name:_____

User:_____

Password:_____

Email:_____

Name:_____

User:_____

Password:_____

Email:_____

Name:_____

User:_____

Password:_____

Email:_____

Name:_____

User:_____

Password:_____

Email:_____

Name:_____

User:_____

Password:_____

Email:_____

Name:_____

User:_____

Password:_____

Email:_____

Name:_____

User:_____

Password:_____

Email:_____

Name:_____

User:_____

Password:_____

Email:_____

Name:_____

User:_____

Password:_____

Email:_____

Name:_____

User:_____

Password:_____

Email:_____

Name:_____

User:_____

Password:_____

Email:_____

Name:_____

User:_____

Password:_____

Email:_____

Name:_____

User:_____

Password:_____

Email:_____

Name:_____

User:_____

Password:_____

Email:_____

Name:_____

User:_____

Password:_____

Email:_____

Name:_____

User:_____

Password:_____

Email:_____

Name:_____

User:_____

Password:_____

Email:_____

Name:_____

User:_____

Password:_____

Email:_____

Name:_____

User:_____

Password:_____

Email:_____

Name:_____

User:_____

Password:_____

Email:_____

Name:_____

User:_____

Password:_____

Email:_____

Name:_____

User:_____

Password:_____

Email:_____

Name:_____

User:_____

Password:_____

Email:_____

Name:_____

User:_____

Password:_____

Email:_____

Name:_____

User:_____

Password:_____

Email:_____

Name:_____

User:_____

Password:_____

Email:_____

Name:_____

User:_____

Password:_____

Email:_____

Name:_____

User:_____

Password:_____

Email:_____

Name:_____

User:_____

Password:_____

Email:_____

Name:_____

User:_____

Password:_____

Email:_____

Name:_____

User:_____

Password:_____

Email:_____

Name:_____

User:_____

Password:_____

Email:_____

Name:_____

User:_____

Password:_____

Email:_____

Name:_____

User:_____

Password:_____

Email:_____